Eating Disorders

Don Nardo

KIDHAVEN PRESS™

THOMSON

GALE

San Diego • Detroit • New York • San Francisco • Cleveland
New Haven, Conn. • Waterville, Maine • London • Munich

THOMSON
$*$ ™
GALE

© 2003 by KidHaven Press. KidHaven Press is an imprint of The Gale Group, Inc.,
a division of Thomson Learning, Inc.

KidHaven™ and Thomson Learning™ are trademarks used herein under license.

For more information, contact
KidHaven Press
27500 Drake Rd.
Farmington Hills, MI 48331-3535
Or you can visit our Internet site at http://www.gale.com

LIBRARY OF CONGRESS CATALOGING-IN-PUBLICATION DATA

Nardo, Don, 1947–
  Eating disorders / By Don Nardo.
    p. cm.—(Understanding issues)
Includes bibliographical references and index.
Summary: Discusses the causes, dangers, and treatment of binge eating, bulimia,
and anorexia.
    ISBN 0-7377-1384-4 (hbk. : alk. paper)
    1. Eating disorders—Juvenile literature. [1. Eating disorders.] I. Title. II. Series.
RC552.E18 N37 2003
616.85'26—dc21

2002013943

Printed in the United States of America

Contents

Chapter One

Binge Eating and Bulimia

Eating disorders are medical conditions that involve serious disturbances in people's eating habits. Most often those suffering from these disorders either overeat or eat too little. And the result is often physical or emotional problems, or both.

Doctors and other experts recognize three major eating disorders. They are known as **binge eating**, **bulimia**, and **anorexia**. Millions of people in the United States suffer from these disorders. Each has certain **symptoms**, or signs and patterns of behavior, that make it different from the others. Yet all three are parts of the same general pattern of disordered, harmful eating. And one disorder can and often does lead to another.

Huge Amounts of Food

For example, all bulimics and anorexics either begin as binge eaters or engage in binge eating from time to time. Binge eaters take in very large amounts of food in a single sitting. They tend to eat too many fattening foods or to eat too much in general. As a result, they are overweight or afraid of becoming overweight.

A binge eater most commonly binges at least twice a week for several months or more. During binges, he

Binge eaters like this young woman consume huge amounts of food at one time.

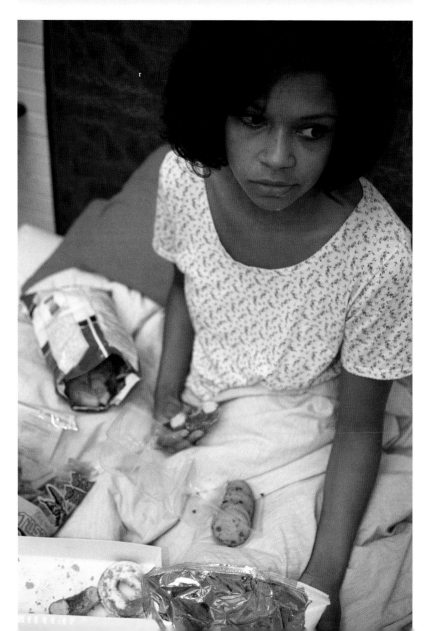

or she usually eats huge amounts of sweets and other **high-calorie foods**. These can include ice cream, cookies, doughnuts, potato chips, cheeseburgers, or anything else the person finds appealing. The amount of food eaten during a binge can be very large. It is not unusual for someone to finish a gallon or more of ice cream, an entire cake, or two boxes of cereal in one sitting. Some binge eaters report eating as many as ten thousand calories in a single sitting. That is the amount an average person eats in four days.

After a few months, the binge eater often stops bingeing for a few weeks or months. He or she may

Recommended Calorie Allowances

	Age Group	Calories
Children	1–3	1,300
	3–6	1,600
	6–9	2,100
Boys	9–12	2,400
	12–15	3,000
	15–18	3,400
Girls	9–12	2,200
	12–15	2,500
	15–18	2,300

Source: Encyclopedia Americana

Many binge eaters gain weight and find it almost impossible to lose it.

go on a diet to lose the weight gained during the binge. But this almost never works. After losing some or all of the weight, the person begins bingeing and gaining weight again. Some give up on dieting and become **obese**, or grossly overweight.

Harmful Effects of Binge Eating

Binge eating is harmful because repeated weight gain and loss interferes with a person's **metabolism**. This is the series of processes by which the body converts food into energy. Chemical reactions in the body's cells burn food, converting much of it into energy. The body

When binge eaters go back and forth between bingeing and dieting, their metabolisms can slow down.

stores excess nutrients—those it does not need right
away—as fat. That is why a person gains weight when
he or she eats more food than his or her body burns.

When a binge eater goes back and forth between
bingeing and dieting, the metabolism constantly tries
to adjust. The body tries to burn calories at an even
rate. But the repeated changes in weight make this
difficult. This causes the metabolism to slow slightly.
A slower metabolism does not burn calories and burn
fat as quickly as before. So the more the weight goes
up and down, the more the metabolism is thrown off.
And the harder it becomes to lose weight.

Binge eating can also harm people in other ways. Almost all who suffer from the disorder binge in secret.
This is because they are ashamed of their behavior and
do not want others to know about it. They often feel
that they have lost control of their lives. "I was con-

stantly depressed and disgusted with myself," says a former binge eater named Alan. "No matter how hard I tried, I just couldn't seem to stop myself."[1]

A Cycle of Bingeing and Purging

Because dieting usually fails for binge eaters, they remain overweight as long as they continue to overeat. For some of them, the thought of being fat is unbearable. So they may resort to more extreme methods of weight control. This can lead to an even more serious eating disorder called bulimia.

Most bulimics begin as binge eaters. But unlike binge eaters, bulimics **purge**, or get rid of, the food they eat. Most often, purging consists of vomiting the food just eaten.

Bulimics usually binge and purge at least two or three times a week. Some do this several times a day. And almost always, like binge eaters, they do so in secret. Typical was the daily routine of a thirteen-year-old bulimic named Joan. "I started eating a lot about two years ago," she says.

> I ate tons of fast food and stuff like that. . . . It wasn't long before I was gaining weight and I hated it when I looked at myself in the mirror. Then I heard from a friend that if you force yourself to throw up after you eat, you won't gain any weight. . . . So then I started eating even more than before . . . sometimes like two whole bags of cookies at once. Only then I went to the bathroom and threw them

up. This was happening four or five times a week. After a while it got to be such a routine that I didn't even have to stick my fingers down my throat any more. Just standing over the toilet was enough to bring the food up.[2]

Dangers of Bulimia

Bulimia has several harmful physical side effects. First, when bulimics throw up, stomach acids come up with the vomit. Over the course of weeks and months, these

Bulimics allow themselves to enter a harmful cycle of bingeing and purging.

A young woman devours an entire cake. Afterward she will most likely purge it.

acids can cause a sore throat, eat away at the surface of the teeth, and make the mouth and jaw swell. Also, frequent vomiting puts a great deal of stress on the stomach. This can cause severe abdominal pain.

Bulimia also has other side effects. Bulimics commonly feel guilty and depressed about their behavior. They may lie to hide the disorder. They may even try to commit suicide. The words of a sixteen-year-old bulimic named Mary show the unhappiness the disorder can cause: "After a while I became really miserable. Most of all I was upset about lying to everybody in my family about what I was really doing . . . and after a while I began to hate myself."[3]

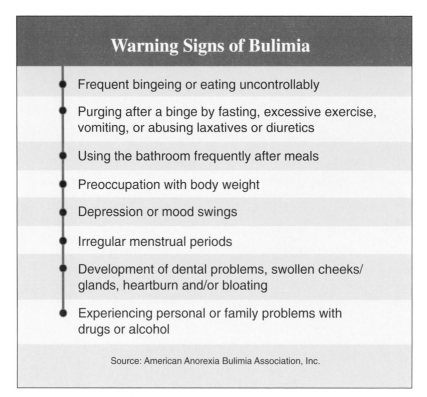

Warning Signs of Bulimia

- Frequent bingeing or eating uncontrollably

- Purging after a binge by fasting, excessive exercise, vomiting, or abusing laxatives or diuretics

- Using the bathroom frequently after meals

- Preoccupation with body weight

- Depression or mood swings

- Irregular menstrual periods

- Development of dental problems, swollen cheeks/ glands, heartburn and/or bloating

- Experiencing personal or family problems with drugs or alcohol

Source: American Anorexia Bulimia Association, Inc.

It is unclear how many people engage in binge eating or suffer from bulimia. Few studies have been done. And most binge eaters and bulimics do not admit their problem. Some studies suggest that 10 to 20 percent of college students surveyed are binge eaters. Other studies show that 10 percent or more of the general female population may be bulimic. Fewer men than women suffer from bulimia. This may be because society places less pressure on men than on women to be thin.

The pressure to be thin may lead some bulimics to feel that purging does not control their weight well enough. They may then turn to the most dangerous eating disorder of all—anorexia.

Chapter Two

The Dangers of Anorexia

Before 1982 most people had never heard of anorexia. That year proved to be a turning point for public awareness of eating disorders. Cherry Boone O'Neill, daughter of singer and actor Pat Boone, published a book titled *Starving for Attention*. In her book, O'Neill told of her long ordeal with self-starvation. She described how she ended up in a hospital. Weighing only eighty pounds, she was near death. Luckily for her, she recovered. And with the help of doctors, she learned to eat normally again.

Cherry O'Neill was the first well-known person to admit publicly that she suffered from anorexia. Then, in 1983, popular singer Karen Carpenter died from heart failure caused by anorexia. And after that doctors and others began writing books warning of the dangers of the disorder.

Obsessed with Thinness

Like people with other eating disorders, those with anorexia begin by having trouble with excess weight. Some may gain only a few pounds. Others become obese. Either way, they have an intense fear of becoming or remaining fat. They react to that fear by dieting. But their diets are much different from the average person's diet. When anorexics diet, they literally starve themselves. Most anorexics take in only about two hundred to five hundred calories a day. That is between one-tenth and one-fifth the amount eaten by an average person.

Because they eat so little, anorexics lose a great deal of weight. And they often become dangerously thin. But although they reject food, they still strongly desire it. So, many anorexics sometimes binge. They may eat large amounts of high-calorie foods, such as ice cream or cookies. Like binge eaters and bulimics,

Popular singer Karen Carpenter, seen here performing, died of anorexia in 1983.

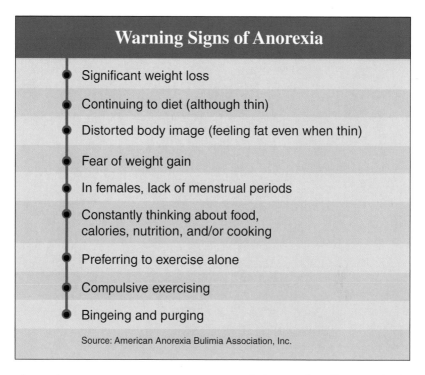

Warning Signs of Anorexia

- Significant weight loss
- Continuing to diet (although thin)
- Distorted body image (feeling fat even when thin)
- Fear of weight gain
- In females, lack of menstrual periods
- Constantly thinking about food, calories, nutrition, and/or cooking
- Preferring to exercise alone
- Compulsive exercising
- Bingeing and purging

Source: American Anorexia Bulimia Association, Inc.

they hope to prevent any weight gain from their binges by dieting or purging. This explains why some bulimics and anorexics go back and forth between the two behaviors. They may starve themselves for a year or more and become very thin. Then they suddenly start eating huge amounts of food and purging it.

Whether they choose starvation diets or purging, anorexics think all the time about being thin. No matter how skinny they get, they still think they are overweight. Anorexics suffer from **distorted body image**. People with this problem do not view their own bodies the same way other people do. When such a person looks in the mirror, she or he sees normal skin and muscles as fat. For this reason, most anorexics do not believe that refusing to eat is a problem.

People with anorexia have trouble seeing themselves as they really are.

While trying to stay thin, anorexics do not rely only on starvation and purging. They may exercise for hours in an attempt to burn calories. They may also use diet pills to curb their hunger. Or they may take **laxatives** and **diuretics** to make themselves go to the bathroom more often. Whatever method they use, their primary goal is thinness.

Most anorexics are girls and young women between the ages of eleven and twenty-two. Older women and men also suffer from anorexia, but it is not as common. Studies of the disorder suggest that about 1 percent of young women in the United States suffer from anorexia. In a high school of two thousand students, about half are girls. And odds are that as many as ten of them may be suffering from anorexia.

Harmful Effects of Anorexia

Doctors have found that anorexic behavior is very harmful. As anorexics eat less and less, their bodies burn and use more and more of their fatty tissues. Eventually, nearly all of their fatty tissues will disappear. But the body still needs nutrients to function. So it starts burning muscle tissue to get those nutrients. And as the muscles grow smaller, the anorexic's weight will drop too. Sometimes, the person's weight drops to seventy pounds or less.

As a result, many anorexics suffer from a lack of proper nutrients, or **malnutrition**. This condition causes many problems, including thinning hair, low body temperature, low blood pressure, and dry skin. Anorexics also often have trouble sleeping. And they run a high risk of sudden death from heart failure. This happens because their bodies are burning muscle tissue in order to survive. The heart is a muscle. And when its tissues get used up, it weakens.

Most anorexics experience other problems too. Nearly all anorexics feel nervous, guilty, and depressed. Some commit suicide. Experts say that 15 to 20 percent of those who suffer from anorexia eventually die from malnutrition, heart failure, suicide, or other causes related to the disorder.

A Young Woman's Story

Most anorexics progress from overeating and weight gain to dieting, often to binge eating, and finally to starvation. Typical, according to one expert, is the case of a young woman named Lynn.

> She was an excellent student, usually making all A's. . . . Lynn had been a popular child

Some anorexics attempt to stay thin by exercising for hours each day.

Women suffering from anorexia think they are fat no matter how many inches they lose.

throughout childhood, but was somewhat shy. Also, she had always been a little overweight, something which her parents had often criticized. Her problems related to anorexia can be traced back to about age 14. At [that] time, she was approximately 15 pounds overweight at about 130 pounds. She began dieting with some of her friends and took up jogging as a form of exercise. . . . She was able to lose 15 pounds in about two months by eating only once per day and jogging from 2 to 5 miles per day. She was very pleased with herself and received many compliments from friends, family, and teachers.[4]

Then Lynn tried to begin eating normally again. She quickly gained a few pounds, which worried and upset her. It worried her so much that she returned to eating only once a day. Eventually, all she thought

Some anorexics are so worried about gaining weight that they weigh themselves again and again.

about was food. And one day she started bingeing on high-calorie foods. Because this behavior upset her more than ever, she exercised for hours every day. She also began taking laxatives on a daily basis.

By the time she was seventeen, Lynn felt disgusted with herself because of her frequent bingeing. At that point, she decided the best way to control her weight was simply to stop eating. For months she ate fewer than four hundred calories per day. And her weight quickly dropped. Her parents took her to a doctor, who diagnosed her as anorexic. The doctor tried to help her, but she continued to refuse to eat. Her grades went down and she suffered from severe depression. After another year she finally had to enter a hospital for treatment.

Unfortunately, Lynn's case is not rare or unusual. Each and every day at least a hundred young people with symptoms of anorexia are admitted to hospitals or clinics in the United States. One million to two million more young people are thought to suffer without treatment. Anorexia and other eating disorders represent a much bigger public health problem than many people realize.

Chapter Three

What Causes Eating Disorders?

The scientific study of eating disorders is fairly new. So experts still debate the causes. All agree on one point, though. Eating disorders have no single cause. They have many causes, and those causes may vary from one person to another.

Still, doctors have found that people with eating disorders share certain experiences and feelings. For example, almost always their problems begin with failed attempts to lose weight. So most experts believe that the three disorders share some underlying causes.

Feelings of Depression

First, many people who abuse food say they do so because they are depressed. Depression is a mental state in which a person feels unusually sad. Events of daily life may feel hopeless or overwhelming. Or the person may feel that life has become meaningless. Nearly everyone feels a little depressed at one time or another. But it is temporary and quickly forgotten. For others, depression is a much more serious and lasting condition.

Many causes of depression exist. Some involve chemical changes in the body. Depression is also caused by emotional changes. For example, witnessing sad or tragic events, rejection by family and friends, and loneliness can lead to depression.

Whatever the reasons for depression, sufferers sometimes turn to food to make themselves feel better. This happened to Tony, a binge eater who is also obese. "Every time I got depressed I ate," he says, "even when I wasn't hungry. It took my mind off my

One cause of eating disorders is the extreme sadness brought on by depression.

problems and I felt there was something good out there—food. . . . The more I ate, the better I felt."[5]

Pressures at Home and School

Poor self-image may also lead some people to overeat. Some people see themselves as ugly, worthless, inept, or untalented. They may feel **inadequate**, or unable to measure up to their own or other people's expectations. And they may come to believe that everything bad that happens to them is punishment for that inadequacy. Take the case of Alice, a young woman who suffered from anorexia for several years. "I felt that no matter what I did, it got all screwed up," she recalled. "So

Some young people overeat because they view themselves as unattractive or unworthy.

Parents who constantly urge a young person to eat more or less can trigger food abuse.

what did it matter if I pigged out and got fat? At least I felt better when I was eating."[6]

Still another factor in disordered eating may be pressures from parents. For example, a young woman named Terri feels that her parents helped cause her problem. She was somewhat overweight in her early teens, she says. But she still managed to deal pretty well with food. However, she remembers, "My parents began to constantly badger me about losing weight. I went on diets but they never seemed to work. Each time I gained back even more weight than before."[7] Terri's frustrating pattern of losing and gaining weight led to a more extreme method of weight control—bulimia.

School pressures can influence the eating habits of young people, too. Some young women fear they will be criticized or ignored by other girls if they are not

Many young women worry that boys will not pay attention to them if they are not thin.

thin. They may also fear that if they are overweight, boys will not ask them out on dates. These worries may cause them to adopt harmful eating patterns. Also at school, both boys and girls feel pressure from teachers and parents to make good grades. Such pressures can cause some students to become frustrated or even depressed. And the next step may be to abuse food.

Society and the Media

Home and school are not the only sources pressuring young people to be thin. Society and the media promote this message, especially to young women. Skinny models and movie stars promote diet plans and expensive exercise machines. And movies, magazines, and clothes designers promote the "anorexic look." Almost always, these ads and programs or movies suggest that overweight people are unattractive.

Experts on eating disorders believe that this constant emphasis on thinness can be harmful. It leads some people to diet unsafely, and it eventually leads to eating disorders.

Taking Charge and Achieving Perfection

Added to all of these pressures are the pressures people put on themselves. Anorexics, for example, often feel overly dependent on others and not in control of their own lives. So, an anorexic finally takes charge by refusing to eat. "I don't have any say in most things that happen to me," says an anorexic named Jane. "But *I* control what goes into my mouth. In that respect, *I'm* in charge, not other people."[8]

Anorexics also tend to set high standards for themselves. Most anorexics are high achievers. They strive hard to make good grades, keep their rooms neat, and please others. Many experts believe that dieting and losing weight become part of an anorexic's overall plan to achieve perfection.

These cases show that anorexia and other eating disorders have complex physical,

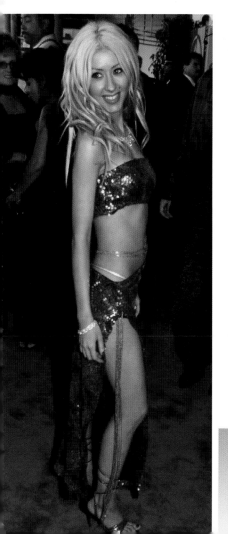

Christina Aguilera poses in a revealing outfit. Teens are easily influenced by the appearance of celebrities.

The fashion industry influences young women by using overly thin models.

emotional, and social causes. Doctors and other medical workers hope to gain a better understanding of these causes. That can happen only, they say, through continued study of eating problems. They know that the more they learn about the causes of binge eating, bulimia, and anorexia, the more effectively they can treat these disorders.

Chapter Four

Treatment for Eating Disorders

In most cases, treating eating disorders is a difficult process. This is partly because doctors still do not fully understand the causes of these problems. They do know, however, that success often depends on the patient. Personality, attitude, and cooperation all play important roles. Marlene, who suffered from anorexia, admitted:

> When my parents took me to see the doctor, I told myself on the way [that] there was no way she was going to force me to eat when I didn't want to. So when I was in her office I just kept nodding at everything she said, but it just went in one ear and out the other. . . . Now I wish I had listened better, cause later on I ended up in the hospital.[9]

There is also a better chance for success if the patient's family and friends are understanding and supportive. "My parents and brother never got mad [at me]," says Nancy, a recovering bulimic. "I don't think I could have done it [stopped bingeing and purging] without them."[10]

Another reason it is hard to treat eating disorders is the importance of food. Food is essential for life. A drug abuser does not have to have drugs to live. So a person who is trying to recover from a drug problem can stop using drugs as part of treatment. Anorexics and bulimics cannot simply stop eating. Instead, they must learn to deal in a healthy manner with the very

A young woman with an eating disorder answers questions on arriving at a clinic.

Sometimes people suffering from anorexia must stay in the hospital for several days or more.

thing that obsesses them—food. And this is almost always very difficult.

Physical Approaches

One common form of treatment for eating disorders is to care for the patient in a clinic or hospital. Most often this is the approach used to deal with people with severe anorexia. Doctors and nurses control the type and amount of food a patient eats so that the patient gains weight. This can be difficult at first. Most anorexics continue to deny they have a problem and refuse to eat. "When I was in the hospital," an anorexic named Anne recalled, "I kept saying I wasn't sick. . . . I looked like a . . . toothpick, but I wouldn't eat anything and even told them I wanted to leave in a really mean voice."[11] In a few very serious cases, like Anne's, the doctors must force nutrients into a patient by inserting feeding tubes.

Another treatment for anorexia involves the use of drugs. **Antidepressants** are commonly used to treat anorexia. These reduce or eliminate the patient's state of depression, which appears to be an important cause of the disorder. Some doctors report success in treating anorexia with antidepressants. A case in point is Marlene, the young woman who ended up in the hospital after refusing to listen to her doctor. "The antidepressants they gave me really helped," she said several months after leaving the hospital. "Before, my spirits were pretty low much of the time, I think because deep down I knew that I really did have a problem. The drugs made it a lot easier to cope with that problem."[12]

Trying to Change Harmful Behavior

Hospital stays, drugs, and other methods have proved helpful in treating anorexia and bulimia. But these approaches alone are usually not enough to bring about a cure. So doctors often use another form of treatment called **behavior modification**. It is a step-by-step process that attempts to modify, or change, a patient's harmful eating behavior. The doctor and patient decide together on a list of goals. For an anorexic, these might include eating all the food on the plate during each meal or gaining a certain amount of weight each week. Anne, the anorexic who had to be fed through a tube while in the hospital, eventually agreed on such basic goals. "I

promised to try and put on at least two pounds a week," she said. "Sometimes I did even better than that, which made the doctor and my parents very happy."[13]

For a bulimic, one obvious goal is to keep from purging after eating. Another is to replace a binge with several small, healthy meals. Typical goals for binge eaters are to eat more slowly, to drink water before meals, and to leave food on the plate at the end of each meal.

Once such goals have been set, the next step is to reward positive behavior. Each time the patient achieves a specific goal, she or he receives a reward. Most often

A doctor counsels a patient who has been admitted to a hospital.

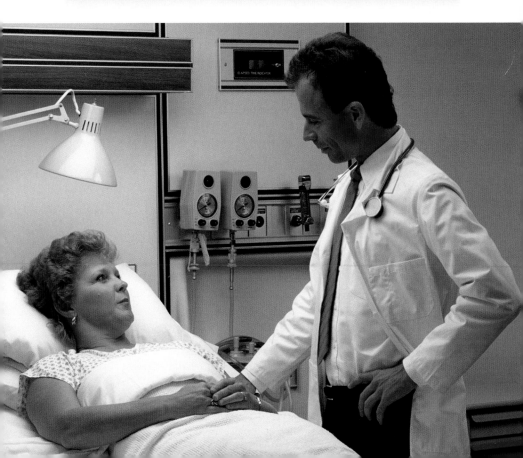

this takes the form of a privilege. For example, the patient might be allowed to take part in certain social activities. In both Marlene's and Anne's cases, their parents allowed them to use the telephone more often.

After leaving the clinic, hospital, or other controlled setting, the chance exists that the patient might fall back into her or his old behavior. "I was fine for almost four months," says Jerry, who suffered from bulimia. "But then one day I suddenly had this wicked urge to eat everything in sight . . . and suddenly being so bloated made me feel like I needed to get rid of it fast, so I

A recovering patient receives the privilege of making a phone call.

Support groups can help by showing the patient that he or she is not the only one with an eating problem.

did."[14] For this reason some doctors believe that behavior modification is not always effective. Other doctors disagree. They teach each patient to keep a food diary, a daily record of the amount of food eaten. Every few weeks the patient shows the diary to the doctor, who checks to see if progress has been made.

Counseling and Support Groups

Still another kind of treatment for eating disorders is counseling. A doctor or other trained person counsels, or talks to and advises, the patient. The goal is to help the person understand the causes of her or his problem. Knowing the causes may help the person overcome them.

Counseling takes different forms. It may involve private meetings between a doctor and a patient. It might

A nutritionist helps a patient map out a healthy eating plan.

also take place in a group setting. Groups often meet one or more times a week to share personal experiences and concerns. "My experiences with the group made a huge difference,"[15] recalled Jerry, who finally recovered from his bulimia.

> At first I didn't say much. . . . I was afraid of what the others would think. But then, I heard them tell how they did the same things I did. Finally, I opened up. . . . Two of the other [bulimics] held me and said they knew how I felt. I felt I wasn't alone anymore.[16]

Whatever the form of treatment used, the goal is the same: to help people with eating disorders deal with food in a normal, healthy way. Tens of thousands of people have achieved this goal. And they all agree that the first step to recovery is asking for help.

Notes

Chapter One: Binge Eating and Bulimia

1. Alan, interview with the author, Barnstable, Massachusetts, March 1999.

2. Joan, interview with the author, Barnstable, Massachusetts, January 1991.

3. Mary, interview with the author, Barnstable, Massachusetts, December 1990.

Chapter Two: The Dangers of Anorexia

4. Donald A. Williamson, *Assessment of Eating Disorders: Obesity, Anorexia, and Bulimia Nervosa.* New York: Pergamon Press, 1990, p. 42.

Chapter Three: What Causes Eating Disorders?

5. Tony, interview with the author, Barnstable, Massachusetts, March 1999.

6. Alice, interview with the author, Barnstable, Massachusetts, December 1990.

7. Terri, interview with the author, Barnstable, Massachusetts, March 1999.

8. Jane, interview with the author, Barnstable, Massachusetts, January 1991.

Chapter Four: Treatment for Eating Disorders

9. Marlene, interview with the author, Barnstable, Massachusetts, December 1990.

10. Nancy, interview with the author, Barnstable, Massachusetts, January 1991.

11. Anne, interview with the author, Barnstable, Massachusetts, December 1990.

12. Marlene, interview.

13. Anne, interview.

14. Jerry, interview with the author, Barnstable, Massachusetts, December 1990.

15. Jerry, interview.

16. Jerry, interview.

Glossary

anorexia (anorexia nervosa): An eating disorder in which a person regularly starves herself or himself and over time becomes abnormally thin.

antidepressants: Drugs used to treat depression.

behavior modification: A form of treatment that modifies harmful behavior.

binge eating (or compulsive overeating): An eating disorder in which a person regularly eats unusually large amounts of food at one sitting.

bulimia (bulimia nervosa): An eating disorder in which a person regularly eats unusually large amounts of food at one sitting and then vomits.

distorted body image: A condition in which a person does not see her or his own body as it really is.

diuretics: Medications that stimulate urination.

high-calorie foods: Foods that contain large numbers of calories, and are therefore very fattening. Calories are units that measure the amount of heat energy produced when a person digests food. The average person takes in and burns between two thousand and twenty-five hundred calories per day.

inadequate: Unable to measure up to standards set by other people or by society in general.

laxatives: Medications that stimulate bowel movements.

malnutrition: Lack of proper nutrients, brought about by eating too little.

metabolism: The series of processes by which the body converts food into energy.

obese: Grossly overweight.

purge: To get rid of something. People with bulimia purge by vomiting the food they have eaten.

symptoms: Signs or parts of a noticeable pattern of a certain behavior or disease.

For Further Exploration

Books

Cherrie Bennett, *Life in the Fat Lane*. New York: Bantam, 1998. One of the most widely read and acclaimed recent books on eating disorders, written especially for young readers.

Janet Bode, *Food Fight: A Guide to Eating Disorders for Pre-Teens and Their Parents*. New York: Simon and Schuster, 1997. An extremely informative examination of eating disorders and ways to cope with and overcome them.

Molly Hoekstra, *Upstream*. Greensboro, NC: Tudor Publishers, 2001. This fictional story about a young girl suffering from an eating disorder is medically accurate, educational, and well-written.

Carol E. Normandi and Laurelee Roark, *Over It: A Teen's Guide to Getting Beyond Obsession with Food and Weight*. Novato, CA: New World Library, 2001. Provides some good advice to young people on how to avoid, cope with, and/or get help for eating disorders.

Paul R. Robbin, *Anorexia and Bulimia*. Berkeley Heights, NJ: Enslow Publishers, 1998. One of the better general overviews of eating disorders.

Website

ANRED (Anorexia Nervosa and Related Eating Disorders) (www.anred.com). This excellent online resource provides comprehensive information about eating disorders in an easy-to-read format. The more than fifty pages of material are very well organized and up to date.

Organizations to Contact

National Association of Anorexia Nervosa and Associated Disorders (ANAD)
Box 7
Highland Park, IL 60035
(847) 831-3438
www.anad.org

The oldest national nonprofit organization dedicated to helping eating disorder victims and their families. ANAD offers many programs including counseling, a referral service, education and prevention information, support groups, and access to research.

National Eating Disorders Association
603 Stewart St., Suite 803
Seattle, WA 98101
(206) 382-3587
www.nationaleatingdisorders.org

An organization of numerous professionals committed to eliminating eating disorders and body dissatisfaction.

National Institute of Mental Health (NIMH)
6001 Executive Blvd., Room 8184
Bethesda, MD 20892-9663
(301) 443-4513
www.nimh.nih.gov

A national organization devoted to eliminating the burden of mental illness through research.

Index

Picture Credits

About the Author

In addition to his numerous acclaimed volumes on ancient civilizations, historian Don Nardo has published several studies of modern scientific and medical discoveries and phenomena. Among these are *The Extinction of the Dinosaurs*, *Germs*, *Cloning*, *Vaccines*, and *Breast Cancer*. Mr. Nardo lives with his wife Christine in Massachusetts.